Lullingstone Roman Villa

Pete Wilson

Introduction

Beautifully situated in the Darent valley, the Roman villa at Lullingstone was inhabited for more than 300 years, from the late first to the fifth century. Though unremarkable when first built, as the inhabitants prospered the villa-house was expanded and embellished, with an attached bath suite, underfloor heating and eventually a luxurious dining room with fine mosaics. In the second century a future emperor may even have lived here.

Lullingstone's real significance, however, lies with the discovery during mid-20th-century excavations of one of the most remarkable finds from Roman Britain: many fragments of painted plaster which, when pieced together, revealed the existence of a Christian house-church. This unique survival provides some of the earliest evidence of Christianity in Britain. Intriguingly the house-church was built over a cellar in which a pagan cult was practised, possibly at the same time as Christians worshipped in the room above.

By the early fifth century Roman rule in Britain had ended and the villa had been abandoned. Some 500 years later, one of the buildings, a mausoleum, was incorporated into a chapel, which was used until the end of the 16th century. Other than some farm cottages which have since been demolished, the site was then deserted. It was only in 1949 that Ernest Greenfield and Edwyn Birchenough (later joined by Lieutenant-Colonel Geoffrey Meates) began excavations on the site, and the remarkable finds were revealed.

Below: A cylindrical glass bottle with dolphin handles, found in the burial chamber of the temple mausoleum

Facing page: A frosty morning on the river Darent. One of about ten Roman villas built in the valley, Lullingstone contained some of the most spectacular finds

The Tour

The earliest house here, built in about AD 100, was a typical villa shape: a block of rooms with a wing at each end. This structure was added to and changed frequently over more than three centuries. The remains visible today date from all four main periods of the villa's development.

Today, what visitors see over most of the site (apart from the mosaics and cellar) are not the Roman floors. Instead, the levels seen are either the layers on which the floors were built, or, for some of the rooms that had underfloor heating, the 'sub-floor' on which the *pilae* (hypocaust supports) stood.

FOLLOWING THE TOUR

The numbers beside the headings, corresponding with the small plans in the margins, highlight key points in the tour.

▮ HEATED ROOMS

The visible range of rooms was not original to the house, but was built in about AD 275 on the site of a wing which was added to the north side of the house in the mid-second century. Although the new range was narrower than its predecessor, it greatly enhanced domestic comfort as, for the first time, rooms outside the bath suite were provided with a hypocaust, or underfloor heating. There were five rooms, the westernmost being unheated. The furnace (*praefurnium*) was probably in the eastern room, under the modern walkway, but could have been further east. Hot air was drawn through arched openings in the dividing walls below floor level and up flues set into the body of the walls. The wall flues were built using hollow 'box-flue' tiles set end to end; part of a flue survives in the north wall of heated room 3. The faces of these tiles were decorated with incised patterns to aid the keying of plaster that covered the walls. The flues were vented at roof level and served both to encourage a draught and thereby the circulation of warm air and also to heat the walls. The rooms furthest from the furnace would have been cooler, since the air would have lost heat as it travelled through the system. When the hypocaust went out of use, probably in the mid-fourth century, it was filled in and a wooden floor was inserted.

The far, westernmost room was probably used as a kitchen in the early fourth century. We cannot be sure of the kitchen facilities, but they would probably have included an oven and a griddle-like hearth. In the second century there was a separate kitchen building west of the house (see page 21).

Facing page: Detail from the geometrical design separating the mythical scenes in the mosaic floor. The design is based on a series of squares, octagons and crosses filled with various motifs, including hearts and swastikas

THE HEATED ROOMS

1 Possible furnace
2 Heated room 1
3 Heated room 2
4 Arched opening in dividing wall
5 Heated room 3
6 Steps to deep room (see page 7)
7 Unheated room, later kitchen

Above: Mosaic and hypocaust at
Chedworth, Gloucestershire, showing
how a hypocaust was constructed
and a mosaic floor laid above it

The Hypocaust

Pillars of tiles called *pilae* (similar to those in the bath suite) supported the floors. Large square tiles (*bipedales*) sat with their corners on four of the *pilae* and probably supported a floor of *opus signinum* (waterproof concrete incorporating tile fragments, which tinged it pink). A mosaic could have been laid on the concrete, although no evidence has been found of this.

2 DEEP ROOM

From the outset, a feature of the villa-house was a deep cellar or room terraced into the slope of the hill. By the mid-second century this 'deep room' had become the focus for a water cult, with a well in the middle of the floor and a wall-painting of three water nymphs in the niche in the southern wall. This, together with other wall-paintings including depictions of date-palms, suggests that the whole room may have been painted. It is not clear whether it was designed as a cult room from the start. When first built the room had two entrances:

one from the south, via wooden stairs leading down from the verandah on the east front of the building; and another at the west end of its north wall, served by both stairs from the south and a ramp from the north. This probably gave rise to the initial suggestion by the excavator, Lieutenant-Colonel Meates, that the room started life as a cellar.

When the house was extended to the north in the later second century, the only door to the deep room – by now certainly a religious space – was in the north-west corner. It could be reached by steps both from outside the building and from within the northern range. In the later third century, however, this entrance was blocked by a wall that formed part of the new heated northern range. This left the bottom three steps protruding into the room. Access can now only have been from above, possibly via a ladder through a trap door. At this time the niche was filled in, covering up the wall-painting of the nymphs. These alterations appear to reflect a change in the cult practised in the room, with the

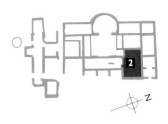

Above: The deep room today
Left: Reconstruction drawing showing the deep room as it may have looked after the house-church was created in the room above. By this date the room could only be reached from above, perhaps by ladder, as shown here
Below: The steps within the north range originally led to the deep room but were blocked in the third century by a new hypocaust wall (on the right)

Religion in the Roman Empire

In Kent and elsewhere people worshipped local deities as well as new gods introduced into Britain from Egypt and the Near East

Above: Gold medallion depicting Constantine the Great (AD 306–37) at prayer, his eyes cast heavenwards
Below left: Gilt-bronze head of Minerva, probably once part of a lifesize statue, from the Roman temple of Sulis Minerva at Bath (first-century AD)
Below right: Bronze head (about 6cm high) found at Felmingham Hall, Norfolk. The Roman god Jupiter is here combined with the Celtic god Taranis (both had power over thunder). The sun rays and moon suggest links with the Roman deities Sol and Luna

In the Roman period, pagan religion had many gods, the main ones being Jupiter, Juno and Minerva. It was also remarkably tolerant. After the conquest of new territories and peoples, the Romans sought to equate their gods with those of the conquered people – hence Sulis Minerva at the great temple complex at Bath, where Sulis, a local deity, was equated with the Roman Minerva. The Imperial Cult – worship of emperors as gods after their death – was also designed to bind conquered peoples to the Empire.

In Kent and elsewhere, people continued to worship local deities, believing that they had to be placated to ensure that daily life was uneventful. At the same time, new gods were introduced to Britain, often from Egypt and the Near East, adding to the diversity. Two cults, however, proved impossible to absorb. Judaism and Christianity were both monotheistic and refused to acknowledge the existence of other deities. Monotheism lay at the heart of Jewish resistance to Rome, and Christians were also regarded as dangerous subversives for refusing to acknowledge the Imperial Cult and were persecuted as a consequence, although with varying degrees of intensity.

When Constantine the Great legalized Christianity in AD 313, it finally ceased to be an underground cult. Its gradual ascendancy in Britain may account for the destruction of some fourth-century pagan temples. Pagan religion did not entirely die out, however: some temples were built or refurbished during the fourth century, for example at Lydney in Gloucestershire. Christianity absorbed aspects of pagan religious practice, not least changing a celebration of the god Mithras to that of the birth of Jesus (Christmas). Similarly the Christian Eucharist may echo a Mithraic feast; and the myths of Mithras and other gods, such as the Egyptian Osiris, incorporate rebirth in their stories.

Left: Photograph of the deep room taken during the excavations, showing the two marble busts (one in two pieces) placed on the deep room steps, near where they were found. One of them is thought to represent Pertinax, a governor of Britain (see page 12)

Below: Small beaker, painted with the word SUAVIS (sweet). It is one of four pots found set into the floor of the deep room (and visible in the photograph above on the left), which may suggest some kind of ritual use. The beaker was made in the Rhineland

veneration of ancestors or the Imperial Cult having superseded that of the water nymphs. Two marble busts, found near the blocked-off steps, appear to be connected with two pots set into the concrete floor nearby.

When the house-church was created above this room, four flint and mortar piers were built against the north and south walls of the deep room. They incorporated slots, some of which retained carbonized wood that had partially survived the final fire in the building (see page 34). Presumably the wood represented timbers providing additional support for the floor of the house-church above. A new clay floor, built at the same time, contained worn coins of the 330s, suggesting that it was laid around the middle of the fourth century. Again, two pots were set in the floor, a deliberate recreation of the previous arrangement, suggesting that the pots were used for something more than storage. They presumably indicate that pagan worship and ritual activity continued, despite the creation of the Christian house-church above. The central well continued to be used: five late fourth-century mortaria (pottery mixing and grinding vessels) were found on the floor nearby. While these could have been used for their intended purpose, they might also have been used as 'balers' for getting water out of the well.

Cellars are known on at least 20 other villa sites, including a further seven in north Kent. One of these, at Chalk, near Gravesend, may also have had a ritual function.

❸ HOUSE-CHURCH

While the cult room is of considerable interest in itself, even more important is the material that it preserved of the debris from the room above. Almost all our knowledge of the Christian aspects of the site derives from this material. The excavators found many thousands of fragments of painted wall plaster which, when painstakingly pieced together, revealed the images that once adorned the walls.

Right: *The reconstructed wall-painting from the west wall of the house-church (now in the British Museum) showing six figures with their hands raised, in the manner of Christian prayer in the Roman period*

Although the surviving elements of the scenes depicted are fragmentary, enough remains to suggest that a large Chi-Rho – an early Christian symbol formed by the first two letters of Christ's name in Greek, *chi* (X) and *rho* (P) – was painted on the south wall. Six near-lifesize standing figures with their hands raised in the attitude of early Christian prayer – the orantes position, still used by priests when saying Mass and by evangelical Christians – were represented on the west wall. A further Chi-Rho appeared on the east wall, and on the north wall there were more figures, as well as pictures of buildings.

The house-church had a narthex, or ante-chamber, which was possibly used by those who had not yet been formally admitted to the Church through baptism and who could not take part in the Mass. This occupied the area of the westernmost heated room of the third-century building, with the former kitchen serving as a vestibule. The painted wall plaster from the ante-chamber provided clear links to the church: it included a Chi-Rho and an alpha and omega, echoing the description of God in the Bible: 'I am the Alpha and the Omega, the first and the last, the beginning and the end' (Revelation 22:13). If access to the house-church was only via the former north range and therefore from an external door, it may have been catering to worshippers from outside the family.

The house-church is a unique discovery for Roman Britain and the wall-paintings are of international importance. They not only provide some of the earliest evidence for Christianity in Britain, but are almost unique – the closest parallels come from a house-church in Dura Europos, Syria.

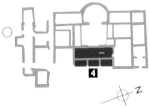

▣ MAIN ENTRANCE/EAST VERANDAH

Given the orientation and layout of the building, it is clear that the main entrance to the house faced the river and as in many villa-houses was located centrally. A verandah ran along its length between the wings, and initially also gave access to the deep room from the south. In its original form

Below: A reconstruction of the east front of the villa-house facing the river, in the fourth century. The main entrance is at the centre of the façade, with the verandah approached by steps

Who Lived at Lullingstone?

We do not know who built the first villa-house. It could have been a rich native who adopted a Roman lifestyle, possibly a noble from the Cantiaci tribe of Kent. Alternatively it may have been an incomer – a retired soldier, successful merchant or administrator.

While most villas are thought to have been occupied by rich and successful Romano-Britons, Lullingstone may have been an exception. The evidence for this rests on the discovery in the deep room of two busts of Greek marble, carved in a style that suggests they were from the eastern Mediterranean. They have been identified as representing Publius Helvius Pertinax, governor of Britannia in AD 185–6 and emperor for three months in AD 193, and his father, Publius Helvius Successus. It has also been suggested that a cornelian intaglio (see page 1) from a ring found here was Pertinax's personal seal. The villa may have been his country retreat while he was governor, which raises the possibility that the villa 'went with the job' and could have been built for one of his predecessors. Estates, however, were regularly bought and sold during the Roman period, and Pertinax may have bought or rented the villa while in post.

Whoever owned the villa, it would have represented the centre of a community consisting of the owner and his family (most, but not all, estates were owned by men), household servants and slaves, as well as estate workers, the latter probably a mixture of tenants, freed men and slaves. The size of the first house suggests a nuclear family, with a limited number of servants and slaves. As the estate prospered and the house grew in size, the household staff would have grown to serve the family's daily needs. We cannot know whether at any time the villa-house was home to a wider family group: some villas, such as that at Darenth further down the valley, appear to have been shared by different branches of the same family, each with their own house. Although there is no evidence of this at Lullingstone, other houses could lie outside the areas investigated, as must most of the farm buildings if it were a typical villa, that is a grand house with a working farm. During the time of Pertinax and possibly other owners with commitments elsewhere, perhaps at Durovernum (Canterbury), a bailiff or estate manager would have overseen the day-to-day running of the estate.

The social circle of a villa-owning family would probably have consisted of family and friends of similar background; many of the neighbouring villa owners might well be related, either by birth or marriage. The family's social and economic ties would have extended as far as Canterbury and perhaps London. Lullingstone's position close to Watling Street and possibly another road running along the Downs to the south would have enabled the owner to attend to business and political duties with relative ease.

While most villas are thought to have been owned by rich and successful Romano-Britons, Lullingstone may have been an exception

Above: Bust, found in the deep room, thought to represent Pertinax, whose governorship of Britain ended with his enforced resignation, apparently because his harsh rule had made the legions hostile to him
Below: Wall-painting from a Roman villa in Trier, Germany, showing estate workers in the fields outside a villa

the verandah possibly had a wooden floor, at least at its northern end. When the steps from the verandah to the deep room were abandoned in the second century, the area was filled with rubble and a solid floor was built across the whole of the original verandah.

In about AD 275 a wall was built linking the frontages of the two original wing-rooms. Two east–west walls in the newly enclosed area may reflect the position of steps from the garden, although no other trace of them has been discovered. Alternatively the east–west cross-walls in the extended verandah could suggest that it had a wooden floor, the cross-walls serving to support the timbers. Another possibility is that the original verandah could have been completely enclosed and used in association with the main reception room, possibly as an audience chamber where tenants and less important visitors were seen. In the later fourth century the verandah appears only to have given access to the domestic parts of the building, the house-church having its own access from the north.

A drain, made of pairs of *imbrices* (half-round roof tiles), was found in the north-east corner of the main reception room (see page 16) running towards the garden, presumably under the surface of the widened verandah. This might relate to the use of the reception room, perhaps for washing the mosaic floors, but it could also reflect difficulties with disposal of water from the roofs of the central part of the structure.

⑤ SOUTH WING

At the south end of the verandah, a wing-room provided symmetry with the north wing. The south wing-room did not have a cellar beneath it, although there was no structural or topographic reason to prevent one from being built. The room's purpose is unknown, in the absence of structural features or groups of finds to provide clues, and indeed its function could have changed over time.

Similarly, the function of the room to the west is unknown, although it did have a white concrete floor, possibly replaced by one of *opus signinum*. Against the south wall was a large pottery jar sunk into a pit. As we see it today, the jar appears to stand proud of the surface, but its rim was at the level of the concrete floor. Geoffrey Meates suggested that the jar may have been a urinal for the convenience of diners, but this seems improbable. The pit itself was filled after the mid-fourth century, on the evidence of coins found there dating from as late as AD 350, and contained several interesting finds, including a bronze 'lion mask' axle cap, a padlock and chain and parts of a glass bowl, as well as quantities of pottery. So whatever the original purpose of the pottery jar, the pit appears to have finished its life as a rubbish pit.

Below: Bronze fitting, perhaps an axle cap, decorated with a lion mask. It was found in the pit in the south wing and buried during the period AD 330–50 or later

Bottom: The large pottery jar found in the south wing, shown in relation to Roman, pre-excavation and modern floor levels

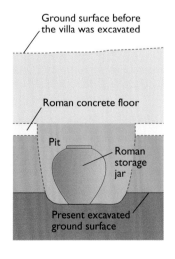

Ground surface before the villa was excavated

Roman concrete floor

Pit

Roman storage jar

Present excavated ground surface

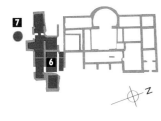

THE BATH SUITE

1 Changing room
2 Cold room
3 Warm room
4 Hot room
5 Hot plunge bath
6 Possible hot dry room
7 *Pilae*
8 Furnace
9 Fuel store
10 Possible later furnace

6 7 BATHS AND WELL

The bath suite as seen today was apparently first built in about AD 150, although the wall of an earlier structure underlies it and could relate to an earlier suite or additional domestic accommodation. The bath suite was more than somewhere to wash: it was also a place for exercise and relaxation, comparable to a modern home gym and social centre for the house. Bathers undressed in the changing room (*apodyterium*), which may also have functioned as a recreation room, and then moved through the baths from a cold room (*frigidarium*) to a warm room (*tepidarium*) and on to the hot room (*caldarium*), which was located next to the furnace (*praefurnium*). A tank (*testudo*) over the furnace provided hot water for the hot plunge bath on the south side of the *caldarium*. The function of the room west of the changing room is less certain, but the fact that it was located close to the furnace and was heated (wall flues to carry heat up the walls can be seen in the east wall) suggests it may have been a hot dry room (*laconicum*), which would provide the bather with an alternative to the damp heat of the main bath suite. Bathers could probably reach the *laconicum* directly from the changing room without going through the steam rooms.

The main bath suite worked like a modern Turkish bath: the gradual increase in temperature opened up pores in the skin and the bather's body was then cleaned using a strigil (a metal scraper) before immersion in the hot bath. Bathers would then return to the changing room through the warm and cold rooms, finishing with a dip in the cold water bath to close their pores. Both the hot and cold baths are often called plunge baths, but were probably no more than 1.2m deep at

most – too shallow for diving. It is likely that the bathers sat in them, often on a built-in step, and poured water over themselves. A modification in the later third century was the addition of a larger cold water bath east of the recreation room. At about 3.5m by 2.5m, this was large enough for bathers to immerse themselves completely, though still not deep enough to dive into.

The water supply initially came from the well outside the southern end of the building. If the water was obtained by hauling up individual buckets, this would have been labour intensive, although a continuous bucket chain, as has been found in London, or a force pump, could also have been used. By the third century the well appears to have gone out of use and was probably replaced by a small aqueduct bringing water from further up the valley. This may have made the larger cold bath viable.

The other major raw material required for the operation of the baths was fuel, probably timber, although charcoal could have been used. The wood could have come from the villa estate, and the need to ensure a long-term supply for both the baths and the heated rooms in the north range suggests that woodland may have been managed through coppicing – timber would have been cut and allowed to regrow.

Use of the baths may have been limited by the labour needed to provide water and maintain the furnace once lit. As well as the owner and his family, estate workers, may also have used the baths, as there was external access to them from the west.

Above: Reconstruction of the bath suite, showing how it may have looked after it was extended in the late third century
Below: The large cold plunge bath, added to the baths in the late third century, was large enough for bathers to immerse themselves

Right: Roman dining scene from the fifth-century manuscript known as the Codex Virgilius Romanus. Believed to depict Dido, Queen of Carthage and the Trojan Aeneas at a banquet in a scene from the Aeneid, the subject is shown in the style of the day, with the larger, important figures reclining on a couch to dine while served by the lesser, smaller figures of their slaves or servants

Below: Large third-century bronze flagon, used for serving drink, found in the mausoleum

8 9 DINING ROOM AND AUDIENCE CHAMBER

As originally built the villa-house had a corridor running all the way along its western side, giving access to the rooms to the east. An earlier ditch running under the corridor at right-angles provides evidence of earlier use of the site. The corridor survived in its original form until the mid-fourth century, when major changes were made to the central part of the house. A central room between the corridor and the verandah was rebuilt, and a new apsidal dining room (*triclinium*) was added to the west, cutting the corridor in two.

The square room east of the *triclinium* may have been the original dining room, or may have served as both a dining room and an audience chamber, where the villa owner could meet tenants and conduct business without visitors having to penetrate too far into the house. Central audience chambers are a common feature of grand houses throughout the Empire.

The design of these rooms, together with the bath suite, demonstrates the extent to which the residents of Lullingstone, if they were not incomers, had adopted Roman social habits. With the addition of the new *triclinium*, both rooms were now provided with fine mosaics. These were designed to face the apse, where the most important guests sat on curved couches, although women may have had high-backed chairs. Other diners probably sat on benches close to the walls of the audience chamber. Small portable tables were provided for those reclining on the couches, and perhaps trestle-type tables for the less important guests. After dinner, the portable tables were cleared away, both to allow guests to see the mosaics – an expression of the host's wealth, taste and learning – and to provide space for after-dinner entertainment. The dining room also afforded fine views across the verandah and over the river.

THE MOSAICS

Techniques

Mosaic floors were made of tesserae – cubes of stone, tile and occasionally glass – and represent the most luxurious type of flooring available. The tesserae at Lullingstone are made from a variety of materials: tile to give red and blue, the latter from the unoxidized core of the tile; chalk (to give white); Wealden sandstone (various colours from purple to near black); and possibly also some imported marble.

However simple the design, the laying of a mosaic was labour-intensive. Simple mosaics could be laid directly *in situ*, but more complex designs were usually prefabricated. The tesserae would normally have been laid on fine mortar overlying *opus signinum*. It is likely that there were regional mosaic workshops (*officinae*), as the same design elements can be seen on a variety of sites. The Lullingstone mosaics pose a problem, however, as they have no close parallels in Britain and are the only fourth-century mosaics known from Kent.

Imagery

Mosaics provided a visible expression of the wealth and good taste of the owners, in which they could display their classical learning and in some cases possibly their religious leanings.

The imagery chosen at Lullingstone is intriguing, as it could represent a disguised Christian message. The main panel in the audience chamber tells the story of Bellerophon, prince of Corinth, on the winged-horse Pegasus, killing the chimera, a fire-breathing she-monster. The story was a well-known myth,

Below: The mosaic from the audience chamber, depicting Bellerophon riding Pegasus and killing the chimera. The central image is surrounded by four roundels (one of which is largely lost) showing the seasons. The main panel designs are of high quality and suggest the work of a master mosaicist; other areas may have been worked by an assistant

Above: *The mosaic from the dining room, showing the abduction of the princess Europa by Jupiter, disguised as a bull. Its inscription suggests that the villa's owners were familiar with Latin literature*

Below: *The mosaic roundel depicting Autumn, wearing a garland of corn*

but at Lullingstone it may also have been intended as an allegory for the triumph of good over evil; and, as the mosaic could pre-date the house-church by a few years, it could be a Christian-inspired message disguised as an expression of classical learning. The scene is surrounded by four roundels containing representations of the seasons (one largely destroyed) – a common feature in Romano-British mosaics.

The other major panel tells the mythical story of the Rape of Europa, who was abducted by Jupiter disguised as a bull. One of the accompanying cupids attempts to intervene by holding on to the bull's tail. A Latin couplet above the image reads:

INVIDA SI TA[URI] VIDISSET IUNO NATATUS
IUSTIUS AEOLIAS ISSET AD USQUE DOMOS

which translates as 'If jealous Juno [Jupiter's wife] had seen the swimming of the bull she would with greater justice have gone to the halls of Aeolus.' The passage alludes to an episode in the first book of Virgil's *Aeneid*, in which Jupiter's wife, Juno, demands that Aeolus, the god of the winds, drowns Aeneas and his fleet at sea; but here it is transferred ironically to Jupiter's abduction of the princess Europa, famously described in Ovid's *Metamorphoses*. Ovid's great poem is written in elegiac couplets, as is the Lullingstone inscription. The allusion to Ovid and Virgil could be a simple play on both poets, perhaps written by the villa owner to display his learning, or it could be taken from the work of a now unknown author. Alternative suggestions are that it hides the owner's name, which could be Avitus (taking the last letter of the first word, and then every eighth letter to the end of Aeolias); or, more intriguingly, that it contains a covert reference to Jesus (taking the first letter in the second line, then every eighth letter and the final letter of the inscription). While the mosaic is broadly of the same date as the house-church, it seems strange that a reference to Jesus would be so disguised, but it could be a way of imposing a Christian message on a pagan scene. Another suggestion is that the mosaic may pre-date the house-church by about ten years, before the owner became openly Christian.

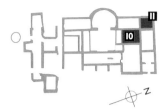

🔟 ⓫ POSSIBLE BEDROOM AND KITCHEN

Between the audience chamber and the north wing is a room which the excavator Meates suggested was a bedroom in the fourth century. This was based on the discovery of two small pits containing small numbers of coins that 'may have been excavated in the floor under the heads of two narrow beds … suggestive of a "barrack-room" layout'. Meates suggested that the occupants were servants due to the apparently restricted accommodation. We cannot be certain that this was a bedroom, however, particularly as the villa may have had a second storey with rooms put to many other uses.

During the second century a separate kitchen block was built west of the main house (see page 21). By the later third century, however, the kitchen may have moved into an unheated room at the west end of the new north range. Meates suggested that this was a kitchen or food preparation room because he found a rubbish pit here containing cooking pots, knives, and animal bones with evidence of knife-cuts. Outside this room was a pit with a clay lining: the clay at the bottom contained a fourth-century coin and the fragmentary skeletons of two ducks, and two geese above them. The geese were buried with their wings extended as if flying, one facing north and the other south – a deliberate positioning which suggests some ritual significance.

In the mid-fourth century the possible kitchen became a vestibule to the house-church, with external access from the north and a door into the ante-chamber to the east.

Above: One of the geese skeletons found in a pit near the kitchen in the north range. The careful arrangement of the bones, which were aligned north–south, suggests that perhaps the geese were sacrificed in connection with the winter and summer solstices
Below left: Two servants preparing food in a pan on a stove, depicted in a second- or third-century relief from the Secundi Tomb at Igl, near Trier in Germany

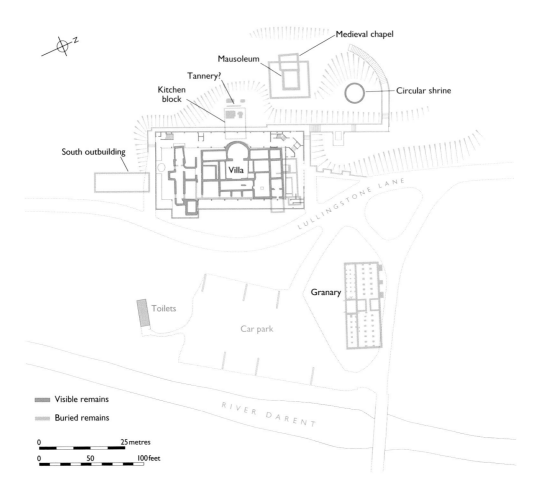

Above: Plan showing excavated buildings outside the villa

Below: The second-century circular shrine, seen during excavation in 1960

BEYOND THE VILLA-HOUSE

Five structures near the house have been excavated, including four non-agricultural buildings and a granary. Of these, only the site of the shrine is marked out, but all are described here.

Shrine and Mausoleum

To the north of the house a second-century circular structure, with the remnants of a floor of coarse red tesserae and traces of red and white wall plaster, may have been a shrine or temple. A fourth-century structure nearby was certainly religious in nature: it takes the form of a Romano-Celtic temple, with a square central room surrounded by an ambulatory. Its primary function appears to have been as a mausoleum, as a large pit at the centre contained a lead coffin, decorated on its lid with scallop shells and a cable pattern. Inside the coffin was the skeleton of a young man. A young woman seems also to have been buried here, although her coffin was damaged when the mausoleum was partially robbed late in the Roman period. An impressive range of grave goods was found with the burials, including pottery and bronze flagons, glass bottles and bowls, two silver spoons, and 30 glass gaming counters on the remains of a gaming board. A bone roundel decorated with the head of Medusa, together with a group of small pieces of bone, may have belonged to a box that contained the game. The mausoleum's remains were incorporated into the late Anglo-Saxon chapel of Lullingstane (see page 34).

Kitchen Block

One of the buildings was a timber-built structure with clay walls, 9.15m by 6.1m, on a platform cut into the side of the valley just west of the house. It was identified as a kitchen because two ovens were found at its western end. The kitchen was built in the second century but may later have been used to process leather for a short time. Alternatively, the 'tanning pit' identified by Meates could have been a latrine, as latrines were often located near kitchens.

South Outbuilding

During the construction of the modern cover building, another outbuilding was discovered. It appears to have been constructed in the later second century and had a timber-built north gable wall 5.8m long, flint cobble foundations to the west and east walls, probably to support a clay wall, and a clay floor. This area was built over in the medieval period; a structure to the east of the villa-house, found by geophysical survey, is probably more recent.

Granary

The main house was only one element of a rich villa farm. A typical villa would have had a variety of farm buildings, as well as accommodation for slaves and estate workers. At Lullingstone, only one certain agricultural building has been excavated: a large, early fourth-century granary or store building, 24m by 10m, located between the house and the river. The floors were raised on stacks of mortared flint, both to deter vermin and to allow air entering through vents in the end walls to circulate under the floor and help keep the contents dry. By the end of the fourth century it seems to have been used as a conventional barn, part of it possibly housing chickens.

Above: Glass counters and dice, from a gaming set found with a wooden board which had been placed on the lid of the surviving coffin in the mausoleum. With them was a bone inlay head of Medusa (top), perhaps from the lid of the box that contained the set

Left: Roman mosaic from Italy showing geese and chickens being fed. In the later fourth century part of the granary at Lullingstone seems to have been used as a chicken run, as it was found to be strewn with eggshells

The Villa Estate

Surplus would have been sold for a profit, funding embellishments to the house and allowing the owner to import luxuries

A typical Romano-British villa would have been the centre of a farming estate, the extent of which may have changed over time. Much land in Roman Britain was tenanted and a big estate might be run by a bailiff with a large number of tenants. Some of them would have worked the home farm that supplied the villa-house, while others worked their own land in return for rent, or perhaps labour services. If much of the estate at Lullingstone was leased out in this way, this might explain the relative lack of agricultural buildings here.

An estate would seek to exploit all the resources at its disposal and Lullingstone's location, typical of the Darent valley villas, gave access to water meadows along the river, with the potential for good arable land in the wider valley, or to the west on higher ground. Woodland was an important resource,

providing raw materials for fences and tools, fuel and probably pannage (grazing) for pigs. Farming would have been mixed, with both animals and crops produced: the excavation provided plenty of evidence of cattle, sheep and pigs as well as hens and other fowl. Surplus would have been sold for a profit, funding embellishments to the house and allowing the owner, whether resident or not, to import luxuries. Flat-bottomed boats could have been used to link the site to the Thames estuary along the Darent, facilitating the transport of goods which was both slow and expensive by road.

Villa estates would have been largely self-sufficient in skills such as blacksmithing, repairing or producing many of the tools and other items that the family and estate needed. Estate owners, however, might buy in products that were not available locally, such as the pottery produced around Cliffe, north of Rochester (Durobrivae), and building stone, such as Kentish ragstone quarried in the Maidstone area.

History

Lullingstone's story
begins with the
construction of a simple
villa-house in about
AD 100. The house was
then continuously
occupied until the fifth
century, expanding as
the owners prospered.
Major changes were
made in the second and
later third century, and
again in about AD 360
when a new dining
room was added with
spectacular mosaics.
At this time too a
Christian house-church
was created above
what had been, and
possibly remained,
a pagan shrine.

THE ROMAN CONQUEST OF BRITAIN

The Roman conquest of Britain began in AD 43 under Emperor Claudius. In that year the army landed in Kent and moved swiftly northwards and westwards, with the Fosse Way, the road from Exeter to Lincoln, marking the western extent of Roman rule by AD 47. Britain was then governed as part of the Roman Empire until the early fifth century.

Under Roman rule, comfortable country houses known as villas – often farms – became a common feature of the countryside. Lullingstone is one of a number of such villas that have been discovered in north Kent, reflecting the area's wealth. Kent was important strategically. Many soldiers would have passed through north Kent as they marched along Watling Street, the Roman road linking London, the provincial capital, with the main entry ports. Several river valleys also provided good communications and gave access to markets for the villa's produce in London and further afield.

THE FIRST VILLA, AD 100–50

Although pre-Roman pottery provides evidence for Iron Age occupation here, Lullingstone's story really begins with the first building for which there is evidence, which dates from about AD 100, some 60 years after the Roman invasion. It was a type of villa commonly found in Britain – a so-called winged-corridor house, built on foundations of local mortared flint, a material visible in churches and houses in the area today. A corridor or verandah linked wings on either side of a central block of living rooms. The house faced the river to the east, and a second corridor ran along the back of the building. The northern wing-room was built over a cellar, which may have been used for storage but, judging from the number of access routes from within the house and outside, may already have been in use as a cult room, as it is known to be from the later second century. Much of this structure is obscured by later alterations. Early in

Above: A gold coin of Claudius, showing his triumphal arch in Rome inscribed DE BRITANN (referring to his victory over the Britons) and surmounted by a statue of Claudius on horseback

Below: The earliest known building at Lullingstone, dating to about AD 100, consisted of a block of at least four main living rooms fronted by a corridor, with protruding wings at either end and a cellar under the north-eastern wing

Facing page: One of the figures from the house-church wall-painting, with arms outstretched in prayer

Roman Kent

From Richborough
and Dover, both
major ports of entry,
soldiers would have
marched along
Watling Street, which
crosses the Darent
valley five miles north
of Lullingstone

Kent was pacified within a few years of the Romans' arrival in
Britain, and rapidly came under largely civilian control.
Nonetheless it retained its military importance: during the second
century the headquarters of the *classis Britannica* (British fleet)
was at Dover, and in the third and fourth centuries four of the
ten major coastal forts known as Saxon Shore forts were in
Kent (Reculver, Richborough, Dover and Lympne). Richborough
and Dover, both on the coast 70 miles away from Lullingstone,
were major ports of entry, and from either port soldiers would
have had to march along Watling Street (the modern A2), which
crosses the Darent valley five miles north of Lullingstone.
Watling Street, like all major Roman roads, was intended
primarily to serve the needs of the army and administration.

Lullingstone lay within the *civitas* (Roman administrative unit) of
the Cantiaci tribe, whose capital was at Canterbury (Durovernum).
According to Caesar – who had led armies to Britain in 55 and
54 BC, but did not stay – four tribal rulers held power in Kent
(Cantium) in pre-Roman Britain. The Cantiaci may have been the
dominant group, or a Roman amalgamation of pre-existing tribes.

The Villas of the Darent Valley

Most of the 60 known and suspected villas in Kent are in the
north of the county. They are in three main groups: focused along
the line of Watling Street between Canterbury and Rochester;
in the Medway valley; and in the Darent valley, where there may
have been as many as ten villas in addition to Lullingstone.

Of the Darent valley villas, Darenth Court, four miles from
Lullingstone, is one of the largest found in the country, and

*Below: North Kent in the Roman
period, showing roads, rivers, towns,
villas and other settlements
mentioned in the text*

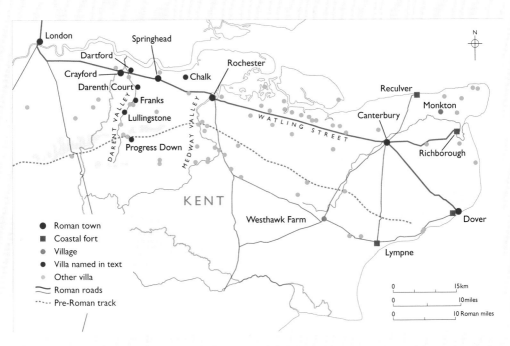

Roman town
Coastal fort
Village
Villa named in text
Other villa
Roman roads
Pre-Roman track

demonstrates what might be expected from a luxurious family home and farm complex. The domestic quarters lie around a large courtyard and incorporate baths, a possible guest house and a swimming pool. There was also an aisled building, which possibly housed a bailiff and workers, as well as a separate bath-house, probably also for their use. The Franks villa at Farningham was, like Lullingstone, occupied from the first to the fifth century and there is evidence for a further two possible villas in Farningham parish, although their histories are less well understood. There are also three possible villas at Otford, one of which, Progress Down, produced an Iron Age brooch as well as evidence that it was occupied throughout the Roman period. Another villa at Dartford was demolished in the third century.

Other Settlements

The nearest settlements of any size were about ten miles away from Lullingstone on Watling Street and are often described as 'small towns'. Springhead (Vagniacis), in the Ebbsfleet valley, was the location of a major religious complex with at least seven temples, and, like Lullingstone, seems to have been occupied before the Romans arrived. Unlike Lullingstone and other neighbouring villas, which were at their height during the fourth century, Springhead declined after the second century, perhaps because by then across Roman Britain surplus money tended to be invested in villas and rural shrines rather than towns. Crayford (probably Noviomagus), to the north-west, is less well known, although the discovery of late Iron Age pottery in the area suggests pre-Roman settlement here too.

Towns and villas were only two elements of the landscape. There were also roadside villages, such as the large one found at Westhawk Farm near Ashford, and one at Monkton on the Isle of Thanet. Both towns and roadside settlements were centres for many crafts and industries. There were also many farmsteads, usually timber-built and farmed either by tenants of a bigger estate or by an individual landowner.

Above: The wall-painting of three water nymphs in a niche in the cult room, which was later filled in, apparently reflecting a change in the type of cult practised here

Below: By the late second century a bath suite had been added to the south of the house, as well as further domestic rooms to the north, which are no longer visible. By now, if not earlier, the cellar was being used as a pagan cult room, and a circular shrine and separate kitchen block had been built north-west and west of the house respectively

the second century a circular building, possibly a shrine, was built to the north of the house and there may also have been a bath-house, although no certain evidence of it has been found. An early wall faced with *opus signinum* (pink waterproof concrete) on the southern side of the villa, and pre-dating the known bath suite, may be part of it.

EXPANSION, AD 150–275

In the second half of the second century the simple winged-corridor house was enlarged, suggesting that the owners had become more prosperous. A bath suite was built to the south, separated from the main house by a corridor with an external doorway at its western end, which suggests that the bath suite was used by people other than the immediate family of the owner. Its position may have been determined by the site of an earlier bath-house and also by a water supply represented by the well to the south. Additional rooms were built on the northern side of the villa-house, with a wing room echoing the eastern façade of the cold plunge bath and almost restoring the symmetry of the frontage.

By this date the cellar was being used as a cult room, probably relating to a water deity or the veneration of water nymphs. The room had wall-paintings, including a picture of three water nymphs in a niche, which was protected from damage when the niche was later filled with stone and mortar.

The two entrances into the cult room from within the house and the east verandah were blocked, and access was now only by steps at the north-west corner of the room, which were in turn reached by three sets of steps. Two of these gave access from outside the building on the western and eastern sides, while the third originated within the new northern range. The external access suggests that people from outside the immediate family – perhaps fellow members of the local elite, workers from the estate, or both – were

Villa Building in Britain

The classic villa-house was designed for living in the Mediterranean area. While villa-type houses in Britain are recognizably part of the same architectural tradition – it would be easy to envisage transplanting Fishbourne Palace from West Sussex to the shores of the Mediterranean – adaptations to the British climate can be seen. Unlike in the Mediterranean, where ensuring a good water supply could be difficult, villa builders in Britain faced the opposite problem: excessive amounts of rain.

So, whereas many bath-houses in the Mediterranean region, such as the 'Hunting Baths' at Lepcis Magna, had roofs with round vaults, it is more likely that in Britain a vault – if there was one – would have been covered with a waterproof roof made of tiles, stone slabs or wooden shingles. Equally, the shaded open courtyards which might be enjoyed in Italy, Spain or north Africa would have had limited appeal in an English winter.

The structure at Lullingstone evolved over time, but would have reflected the materials available. Kent lacks good building stone, so walls of mortared flints, plastered or rendered over, are the norm, although much of the superstructure could have been timber-framed and perhaps limewashed. What little building stone is known from the site comes from architectural features, such as the stone column from the deep room. It is possible, however, that originally more stone was used, particularly where it would have been visible, and that it was taken for reuse elsewhere once the villa-house was abandoned.

Roofing materials were not recorded in the excavation report in any quantity, possibly because they were not thought to be particularly interesting, but it may be that the roofs were removed for reuse elsewhere. The roof of the southern aisle of the granary was in part replaced with tiles in the fourth century – perhaps from elsewhere on site.

The shaded courtyards which might be enjoyed in Italy, Spain or north Africa would have had limited appeal in an English winter

Above: This first-century wall-painting from Pompeii shows a typical Mediterranean villa with a colonnaded verandah, central entrance and wings. The same basic design was transferred to Britain, though adapted to suit the very different climate

Above: One of the two lifesize busts found in the cult room. This one is thought to represent Publius Helvius Successus, father of Pertinax (see page 12). The presence of the busts together with pots for offerings may suggest the use of the room for the veneration of ancestors or the Imperial Cult

Below: In the late third century the northern range was replaced with a series of heated rooms and additions were made to the bath suite, including a larger cold plunge bath

involved in the cult practised here. At some point during the third century the entrance steps were blocked, and two marble busts appear to have been placed on or near the lowest steps that protruded into the room. Access to the cult room was now only from above, presumably through a trap door, and the busts suggest that the emphasis changed to the veneration of ancestors, or the Imperial Cult.

RESHAPING THE VILLA, AD 275–350

In the later third century the northern range was demolished and replaced with a narrower range of five rooms, three of which incorporated an underfloor heating system; hot air was also drawn through wall flues, heating the walls as it rose to the roof. Other than the bath suite, these were the only rooms with underfloor heating. Other rooms must have been heated by braziers. Underfloor heating reflects the prosperity of the owners, as such a system demanded labour and resources.

The eastern verandah was now either widened, or converted into an audience chamber, with a new verandah to the east incorporating steps from the garden. The bath suite was modified, the main change being the provision of a larger cold plunge bath beside the original one, which may now have been used as a cistern. This change may have related to a modification of the water supply, with the labour-intensive well being replaced by an aqueduct drawing water from higher up the valley. A new furnace or *praefurnium* was also built, possibly replacing a smaller structure. This room would have sheltered those operating the furnace, but could also have been a fuel store, ensuring a ready supply of dry timber.

Two external buildings, the granary and the mausoleum, date to this period. The granary is one of the largest known from a civilian site in Roman Britain, and the mausoleum, in which a young man and woman were buried, is an ostentatious, if pious, expression of wealth.

THE CHRISTIAN VILLA, AD 350–425

Around the middle of the fourth century some remarkable changes took place that distinguish Lullingstone from many of the other villas known in Roman Britain. First, the central core of the house was radically altered when an apsidal dining room or *triclinium* was built across the line of the western corridor, splitting it in two (page 16). This dining room, with its attached audience chamber, and the mosaics within the rooms (page 17), demonstrate the increasing prosperity of the villa.

Even more remarkable were the changes above the deep room involving the creation of a house-church (page 9). While the dining room, mosaic floors and wall-paintings are the kinds of embellishments to be expected in an elite residence such as Lullingstone, the wall-paintings in the house-church set the villa apart, as they are the only known paintings from a villa in Roman Britain that contain clear Christian symbolism.

These paintings represent an overt statement of Christianity by Lullingstone's owners. Persecution of Christians officially ceased after the adoption of Christianity by the Emperor Constantine in AD 313. The fact that the paintings date from some 40 years after this could mean that the owners of Lullingstone may not have adopted Christianity until well after it was officially accepted. Alternatively, if the mosaics do contain coded Christian inscriptions and depict the Christian message of the triumph of good over evil (see page 18), Christians here could have feared the return of intolerance and persecution, despite sanction of their religion, and so preferred to worship covertly for a time. Another possibility is that they may only have acquired the wealth to embellish their house at a later date.

Perhaps almost as remarkable as the discovery of the house-church is the possibility that pagan worship may have continued in the cult room below. This may indicate that the family were hedging their bets, trumpeting their apparent

Above: *Detail of the scallop-shell decoration from the end of the surviving lead coffin of a young man, found in the mausoleum*
Below: *This ceramic jug, manufactured near Oxford, was found in the mausoleum, where it had been placed beside one of the coffins*
Below left: *In the later fourth century the house was modified again, with an apsidal dining room added at the heart of the building. At about the same time some of the domestic rooms in the northern part of the building were converted into a house-church*

Early Christian Worship

The Lullingstone wall-paintings and finds elsewhere provide hints about how early Christians worshipped

We know little of how early Christians worshipped in Britain, but hints are provided by the Lullingstone wall-paintings and finds elsewhere. A villa at Hinton St Mary, Dorset, may also have been a place of Christian worship: a fine mosaic was found there depicting a figure generally accepted to be Christ. Near Hinton St Mary is another villa, at Frampton, where mosaics tell the story of Bellerophon and include a Chi-Rho.

Possible Roman-period churches have been discovered at a number of sites in Britain: at towns such as Colchester, Silchester and Lincoln; in the northern frontier forts of Housesteads, South Shields and Vindolanda; at former pagan temple sites, including Brean Down and Lamyatt Beacon (Somerset) and Uley (Gloucestershire); and within the Saxon Shore fort at Richborough. At the latter a stone and tile baptismal font has been found, of a type also known at Ivy Chimneys (Essex), Icklingham (Suffolk) and Silchester. Both the Richborough and Silchester examples lay outside the churches.

Much of the evidence for Christianity in Britain is in the form of portable objects. Unique to Britain is a series of lead tanks carrying Christian symbols and imagery which probably represent baptismal fonts: one, from Walesby (Lincolnshire), probably depicts a baptism. Other objects bearing Christian symbols include spoons, rings, brooches, cups and other metalwork.

Although not all late Roman inhumation burials orientated west–east can be seen as representing Christians, Christian cemeteries have been identified, such as that at Poundbury, Dorset, where mausolea – one with figured wall-paintings – are known. The Poundbury mausolea, at around 6m by 4m, were smaller than the Lullingstone mausoleum (12.5m by 11.5m), although considerably bigger than the central burial chamber within it.

Above: A fourth-century Romano-British ring from Suffolk, decorated with a Chi-Rho monogram (engraved in reverse)
Right: The central roundel of a fourth-century mosaic from a villa at Hinton St Mary, Dorset. It is thought to depict Christ surmounted by a Chi-Rho, although this interpretation has been challenged

Left: *Reconstruction, now in the British Museum, of the painting of a Chi-Rho from the south wall of the house-church*
Below: *The reverse side of a coin of Emperor Honorius (AD 395–423) showing him trampling on a barbarian. During his reign much of the Western Empire was threatened both by invaders and by usurpers to the throne*

acceptance of Christianity, while trying to keep the old gods happy; or perhaps some members of the family clung to old beliefs in the face of the adoption of Christianity by others. It might also represent an expression of pragmatic Roman polytheism, which accommodated a variety of gods. Such an attitude, however, would have been unacceptable to genuinely devout Christians, whose refusal to acknowledge other gods had been a major factor in their persecution, as it was for the Jews, who were equally defiant in their monotheism.

THE END OF ROMAN BRITAIN

The Roman period in Britain did not end abruptly. The Empire by now had a western capital in northern Italy – Milan from AD 286 and Ravenna from AD 402, rather than Rome – and the eastern part was ruled from Constantinople (Istanbul). In the face of attack from various barbarians, including Goths, Suebi, Vandals and Alans, the Western Empire withdrew troops to defend its core in Italy, but troops were also removed in support of various usurpers who originated in Britain and campaigned on the Continent to become emperor, including Magnus Maximus (AD 383–8), Eugenius (AD 392–4) and Constantine III (AD 407–11). Roman imperial authority was restored several times, but tradition has it that in AD 410 the Western Emperor Honorius (AD 395–423) wrote to the British cities to look to their own defence. While it is now generally believed that Honorius's letter was probably sent to Bruttium in southern Italy, not Britain, such advice would have reflected the realities of the time. Sending aid to a far-off province was not a high priority for a Western Empire faced with invasions of Italy.

A recognizably Roman lifestyle would have continued for some time into the fifth century, but the economic basis had altered. No longer was there a standing army needing

Above: One of many pieces of Roman tile excavated at the villa. In this fragment a dog's pawprints have been pressed into the clay before firing

Below: The Lullingstone bowl, a late sixth- to eighth-century bronze hanging bowl decorated with birds, stags and axeheads, which was found in a Saxon grave near the villa

supplies, and gradually the traders seeking to buy the goods and agricultural produce that had underpinned the preceding economic system disappeared, as did the money economy. Army pay had been the source of most of the money entering the country and this dried up when the army left Britain: coins dating to after AD 395 are not common in Britain, with the mysterious exception of 20,000 coins of AD 395–402 found at the port of Richborough, more than from the whole of the rest of the country put together. Despite this anomaly, it is believed that the monetary economy had largely fizzled out by AD 425 and with it large-scale industries, such as the commercial potteries. Villas and other settlements may have become increasingly dependent on their own resources, probably using more locally made wood and leather containers rather than pottery.

THE END OF THE VILLA

At some point in the fifth century there was a fire at Lullingstone, and the villa-house appears to have been abandoned, if it had not been already. It is unclear when this happened, since no new coins were coming to the site to provide dating evidence.

Once Lullingstone was abandoned and the roof had fallen in – or perhaps tiles had been taken off to be reused elsewhere – plaster would gradually have fallen from the walls, and soil washing down the valley side, with naturally developing compost from vegetation, would have accumulated and over time covered the site. The walls themselves would have been taken down for reuse, or collapsed where they stood. How long this process of decay took is difficult to say, and different buildings may have lasted for different lengths of time. The mausoleum seems to have survived, at least as a ruin, to be incorporated into Lullingstane Chapel, probably in the 11th century. Whether this was simply because the walls were there and could be reused, or because it represented a deliberate 'Christianizing' of a site with lingering pagan associations, is uncertain.

SAXON, MEDIEVAL AND LATER LULLINGSTONE

There are hints of settlement in the valley in the early Saxon period, from the later fifth or sixth century. There are records of 'burial places' which were discovered in 1860 during the construction of the railway line to the north of the villa site, although their exact locations and numbers are unknown. The remarkable Lullingstone bowl, a 'hanging bowl' of intricate workmanship possibly made in Scotland between the sixth and eighth centuries, was found in one of these Saxon graves and points to the high status of some people in the area.

The chapel of St John the Baptist, Lullingstane, is first recorded in 1115, but is likely to have originated before the

Norman Conquest. There is a drawing of it as a ruin in 1769 and it appears to have survived in this condition until at least 1797. A description accompanying the drawing refers to it being 'built with flints and Roman bricks, the west end being chiefly of the latter'. The chapel would have served the medieval hamlet of Lullingstane: burials found on the south side of the chapel during the excavations represent members of its congregation, and medieval walls found over the villa's south outbuilding (see page 21) suggest the location of one or more of the buildings of the hamlet.

Domesday Book records three estates at 'Lolingstone': Lullingstone Ross, Lullingstone Pryforer and Cockhurst. There may also have been a separate estate of Lullingstane, and, rather confusingly, there was also 'Lullingstone Castle' – a name which until about 1740 referred to Shoreham Castle, probably founded in 1068 and in ruins by the 16th century. Lullingstane parish, having been reduced to a population of two families, was combined with Lullingstone in 1412 and the families moved from the hamlet.

Lullingstone House, as it was then, was built in the late 15th century, its fine brick gatehouse surviving from 1497. It was renamed Lullingstone Castle in about 1740. In 1550 the Lullingstane estate was sold to Percyval Hart, who owned Lullingstone, and from then on there was no differentiation between the two. Lullingstone deer park was established in the time of Elizabeth I.

At some point cottages were built in the area of what is now the villa car park. These were demolished around 1914.

Above The 15th-century gatehouse at Lullingstone Castle
Below: Lullingstane Chapel in 1769. The chapel, built partly over the site of the mausoleum, was probably pre-Norman and would have served the medieval hamlet of Lullingstane

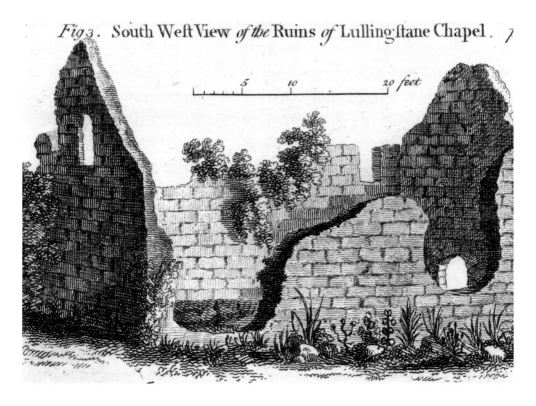

Fig 3. South West View *of the* Ruins *of* Lullingstane Chapel .

Above: Sir Thomas Dyke, second
baronet, the owner of Lullingstone
Castle in the 1750s, when tesserae
from the villa were found
Below: Lieutenant-Colonel Geoffrey
Meates, who became sole director
of the excavation in 1955, overseeing
the cleaning of the mosaics

Facing page: Detail from the
wall-painting of three water nymphs
discovered in the deep room in 1957

DISCOVERY AND EXCAVATION

The Roman villa is first recorded in about 1750, when the
fence around Lullingstone deer park was being renewed,
and holes for posts were dug through a previously unknown
mosaic. These events were reported by John Thorpe in
Custumale Roffense, published in 1788, when Lullingstane
Chapel was also illustrated.

In 1939 members of the Darent Valley Archaeological
Research Group found roof tiles and tesserae from a floor
in disturbed ground where a tree had blown down. The
outbreak of the Second World War prevented further
exploration, but in 1949 the group began excavations that
continued until 1961. Initially the direction of the project
was shared between Ernest Greenfield, an experienced
archaeologist, and Edwyn Birchenough, a classical historian;
they were later joined by Lieutenant-Colonel Geoffrey
Meates, who had recently retired from the Royal Artillery
and was living in the gatehouse at Lullingstone Castle. By
1955 Meates was in sole charge.

The excavations were undertaken with volunteers,
including local people and schoolchildren, and funded by
donations from visitors and occasional grants. The project
was in large part driven by the enthusiasm and commitment
of those involved, while the use of sheeting and carefully
positioned boarding, shielding the site from the neighbouring
public road, ensured that the maximum number of people
paid to visit the excavations and so supported the work.
The quality of the remains and the importance of the
discoveries ensured that the project received widespread

Above: The excavation of the villa attracted much public interest. A platform (right) was built out over the north side of the villa-house to provide a view of the mosaics. In the background, higher up the valley slope, the temple mausoleum is being excavated

Below: Sketch of R J Rook 'Rookie' made by Frances 'Pixie' Weatherhead, one of many she made of people working on the excavation

support from many of the leading archaeologists of the day, and a number of people who subsequently became well-known archaeologists passed through the project.

Essentially the site was dug on a grid system, in keeping with the practice of the time. Trenches were separated by 'baulks' – vertical walls of archaeology left *in situ* – which served two purposes, facilitating movement around the site and perhaps more importantly allowing the vertical faces (sections) through the archaeology to be drawn as part of the site record. The grid seems to have been modified to take account of the shape of the various rooms, and in areas swept away so that the full extent of key features, such as the mosaics, could be seen, aiding both the display of the excavations and the understanding of the site.

In 1956 the Ministry of Works, a predecessor of English Heritage, took over the site with a view to ensuring its long-term preservation and display, with Meates remaining as director of the continuing excavations. The site was taken into state guardianship in 1958 and the cover building opened to the public in 1963. One-time members of the excavation team, Mr and Mrs R J Rook, became the first custodians of the site, their commitment and enthusiasm inspiring their son, (now Dr) Tony Rook, who has researched and published widely on villas and bath-houses.

The discovery of the Christian wall-painting was regarded as so important that in 1956 the Ministry of Works and Kent County Council moved the road that ran over the eastern part of the villa-house to allow the complete excavation of the cellar or deep room.

The Mausoleum Revealed

Jonathan Horne recalls his work on the dig as a teenager:

'I first heard about the villa when I went out with my parents for a Sunday afternoon drive. I was 13 at the time. We walked down to the villa and I asked how to become one of the team. I was told I could come along and camp on the site. So that is what I did, from 1953 to 1963. It was an incredibly rich site. Wherever you dug a hole, masses of stuff came out.

'When I first arrived there was a trench going straight up the hill at the back and I was put to work picking at heavy flints in the thick clay. It was really tough work. One Monday morning, after all the weekenders had gone, I was left alone hacking away. I decided to scrape away at the floor, which was a trampled chalky mess where we'd all been standing, and came across a straight edge. Later we found that this was the west wall of Lullingstane Chapel.

'A man working below me started finding narrow walls, and we didn't know how these related to the chapel. He was also digging up masses of *opus signinum* as well as lumps of lead and some bones. The Colonel took the bones to some expert in London who said 'Mm, these aren't very old'. But as we progressed the next year it was revealed that these walls were a Roman temple, with a tomb underneath. The fragments of lead and bones were from a coffin that had been stolen, but then we discovered another lead coffin that had been squashed flat.

'Usually the senior archaeologist dug in the hole, but near the end of the third season, as I had been there for some time, I was allowed to dig there. It was quite an experience to find all these wonderful treasures – pieces of glass bottle, the two silver spoons, and a big jug. When we found the bronze flagon I could see the top sticking out and the chain still loose, just as it is today.

'I knew, even at the age of 16, that this opportunity of digging out a Roman tomb would never come again. And I was right – it never has!'

'I knew, even at the age of 16, that this opportunity of digging out a Roman tomb would never come again'

Below: Two silver spoons found by Jonathan Horne among the grave goods in the mausoleum
Below left: The surviving coffin being lifted out of the mausoleum by young volunteers. Jonathan Horne is the second from the right

Above: The entrance to the villa cover building today

Below: The villa remains and modern viewing galleries, with the bath suite in the foreground

THE VILLA TODAY

The villa as it is seen today is essentially what was visible in 1963 when the cover building opened. Although only limited further work has been done, our understanding has changed radically. As understood by Lieutenant-Colonel Meates, the villa-house went through a period of abandonment in the third century. He also suggested that there was an open courtyard to the south of the room with the Bellerophon mosaic. Small-scale excavations by Dr David Neal in 1983, which he coupled with careful examination of the wall-joints, have told us much about the sequence and history of the site. Meates's plans of the different phases of the villa have had to be substantially redrawn and elements of the story completely revised. While it is clear that the villa went through changes of fortune, it is no longer thought to have been abandoned and then reoccupied, nor that there was an open courtyard within the villa-house.

Other developments in interpretation include the recognition of imperial connections (page 12), which suggests that the villa might not be a conventional farm complex, but possibly the country retreat of the provincial governor. Such a function could explain the limited range of external buildings found, and could mean that the granary was intended to receive supplies brought up river, rather than being an assembly point for agricultural produce to be sent down river. Given the topography of the site, with most of the buildings set on terraces on the valley side and close to the river, it is possible that further agricultural buildings remain to be found to the north or south of the areas excavated so far.